The Best Book of
Trains

Richard Balkwill

KINGFISHER
NEW YORK

Contents

KINGFISHER
LONDON & NEW YORK

Author: Richard Balkwill
Illustrators: Tom Connell, Chris
Forsey, Peter Bull, Mike Atkinson,
Richard Draper

Drawings on p. 12 top right and
p. 13 top left © Venice Simplon-
Orient-Express Limited

Distributed in the U.S. by Macmillan,
175 Fifth Ave., New York, NY 10010
Distributed in Canada by H.B. Fenn and Company Ltd.,
34 Nixon Road, Bolton, Ontario L7E 1W2

Library of Congress Cataloging-in-Publication Data
Balkwill, Richard.
    The best book of trains / by Richard Balkwill.—
    1st ed.
        p.cm.
    Summary: Introduces all sorts of trains from around
the world, covering different types of trains, how they
are constructed and how they run, who drives them,
and more.
    1. Railroads—Trains—Juvenile literature.
[1. Railroads—Trains.]
TF148.B24   1999
625.'1—dc21   99-12757   CIP

ISBN: 978-0-7534-6171-6

Kingfisher books are available for special promotions
and premiums. For details contact: Special Markets
Department, Macmillan, 175 Fifth Avenue, New York,
NY 10010.

For more information, please visit
www.kingfisherbooks.com

Printed in Taiwan
10 9 8 7 6 5 4 3
3TR/0310/SHENS/PICA/126.6MA/F

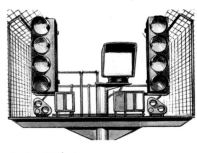

The first railroads

More than 250 years ago, railroads in Europe were being built to carry material **from mines.** At first, these rails were made of flat stones laid in the ground. Loaded wagons could then run down a hill by force of gravity. Workers had to steer them to keep them from running off the rails. Soon, metal rails were laid down, and flanges, or lips, on either side of the wheels kept the wagons on the rails. The distance between the rails was known as the gauge. By the early 1800s, inventors had found a way to power engines using steam from water heated by coal fires.

Horse power
Before the invention of steam engines, horses were often used to pull wagons along rails.

The first passenger railroad
By 1830, the English cities of Liverpool and Manchester were connected by rail. The 30-mile line was the first double-tracked railroad with passenger trains running on a regular schedule. The trip took around two hours.

Catch me who can
This was built in 1808 by Richard Trevithick, engineer of the world's first working steam locomotive in 1804.

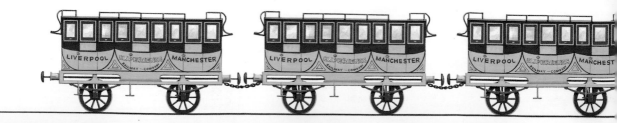

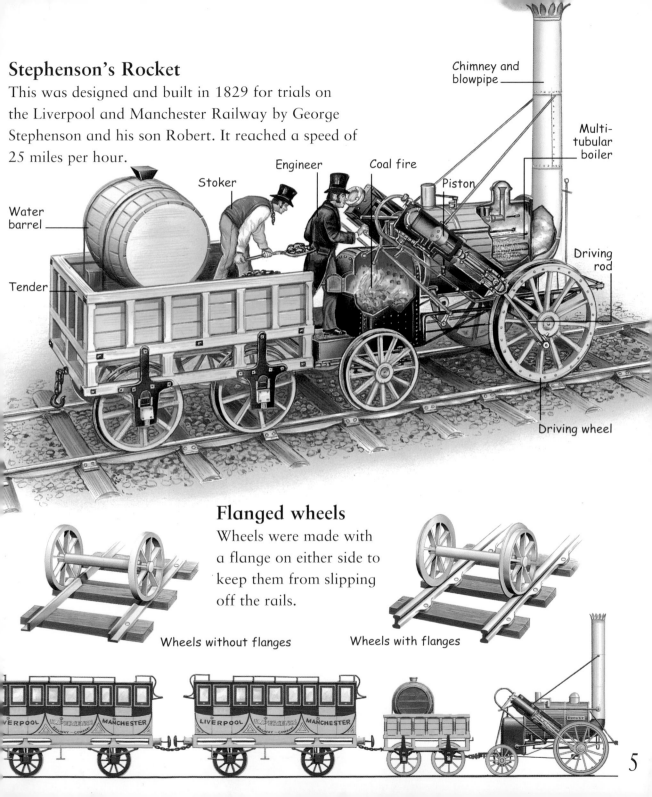

Stephenson's Rocket

This was designed and built in 1829 for trials on the Liverpool and Manchester Railway by George Stephenson and his son Robert. It reached a speed of 25 miles per hour.

Chimney and blowpipe

Multi-tubular boiler

Engineer

Coal fire

Piston

Stoker

Water barrel

Driving rod

Tender

Driving wheel

Flanged wheels

Wheels were made with a flange on either side to keep them from slipping off the rails.

Wheels without flanges

Wheels with flanges

LIVERPOOL EXPERIENCE MANCHESTER RAILWAY COMPANY

LIVERPOOL EXPERIENCE MANCHESTER RAILWAY COMPANY

ROCKET

A faster way to travel

In the 1850s, train travel completely changed the way people moved around the country. Before that, coaches drawn by teams of horses often took four days to travel 150 miles. In the winter, the rough roads might be flooded or blocked by fallen trees. The new trains carried people the same distance in around four hours.

Paddington Station

This station, in London, England, was designed by English engineer Isambard Kingdom Brunel and opened in 1854. From here, passengers could travel the 195 miles to Exeter on the Great Western Railroad.

The roof at Paddington Station was made up of great arches

Open-top cars

In the 1840s, rich people traveled in their own covered cars. The poor had to stand in open cars in the wind and rain, and smothered in smoke from the engine. By 1850, railroads provided cars for second and third class travelers with hard benches and a roof.

Porters secured baggage to the top of the train

In 1869, the two lines met at Promontory, Utah where the last spike was driven in

CALIFORNIA

Rocky Mountains

Green River

Sacramento

NEVADA

UTAH

Salt Lake City

Crossing the continent

The first railroad to cross an entire continent was built in the United States. It was completed in 1869, linking the country from coast to coast. The new railroad system allowed settlers to move all across the country in search of new land. But the track ran through territory that belonged to Native Americans, who called the train the "iron horse." They often attacked the railroad builders in defense of their land.

Steam power

This steam engine was typical of the kind used on the new railroad. It weighed about 40 tons and could travel at up to 19 miles per hour.

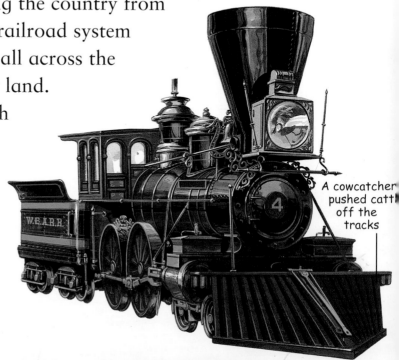

A cowcatcher pushed cattle off the tracks

W.E.A.R.R.

Meeting in the middle

The Central Pacific started laying track eastward from Sacramento, California, while the Union Pacific laid track westward from Omaha, Nebraska. When finished in 1869, the line ran for 1,078 miles.

The Native Americans fought to protect their homeland

WYOMING

COLORADO

Cheyenne

North Platte

KANSAS

Omaha

Previously built railroad lines connected the new line to the East Coast

Bridges of iron and wood were built to cross valleys

Many of the workers were immigrants

Heavy work

Teams of workers laid track by fixing iron rails to wooden sleepers with spikes. In 1869, a record 10 miles of track was laid in one day by a team of 800 men.

Steam engines

Until the 1950s, most passenger and freight trains were hauled by steam locomotives. Coal (and sometimes oil) was burned to heat water and make steam at high pressure. This moved a piston back and forth, which drove the wheels. The advantage of these engines was the simplicity of their design. But they generated a lot of steam and smoke and had to carry their own supply of fuel on board. With the arrival of diesel and electric engines, the great age of steam came to an end.

Steam in China

In China, where there is plenty of coal, steam locomotives were being built until 1995. Engines like this one are still widely used to haul both freight and passenger trains.

Puffing uphill

In the Rocky Mountains of Colorado, old steam engines are still used to haul tourist trains on the Durango to Silverton line.

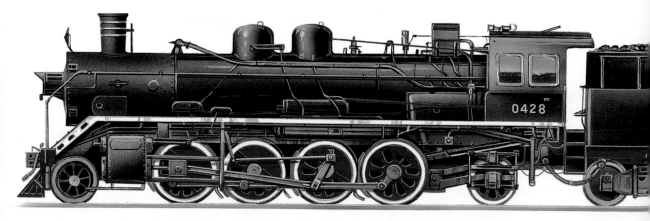

0428

Big Boy

The world's largest and most powerful steam engine is the 500-ton Big Boy. Twenty-five of these were built in the 1940s to haul freight trains in Utah.

Mallard

The world's fastest steam engine is the Mallard. In July 1938, this streamlined locomotive reached a speed of 125 miles per hour between Grantham and Peterborough in England. It was eventually retired from service in 2007.

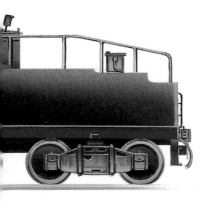

Traveling in luxury

During the 1850s, railroad companies began to build more comfortable passenger cars, especially in the U.S.A. and Europe.
Many long-distance trains were now equipped with heating and lighting. In 1865, U.S. businessman George Pullman built the first sleeping car, which also had a bathroom. His name has been used to describe luxury cars for dining and sleeping ever since. This form of travel became very popular for those who could afford it. Today, many of the cars have been restored for use by tourists.

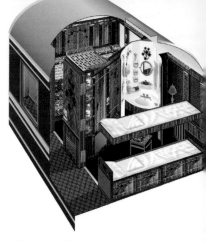

By night
Bunkbeds fold down from the walls. This compartment on the Venice Simplon-Orient-Express also contains a sink and hanging space for clothes.

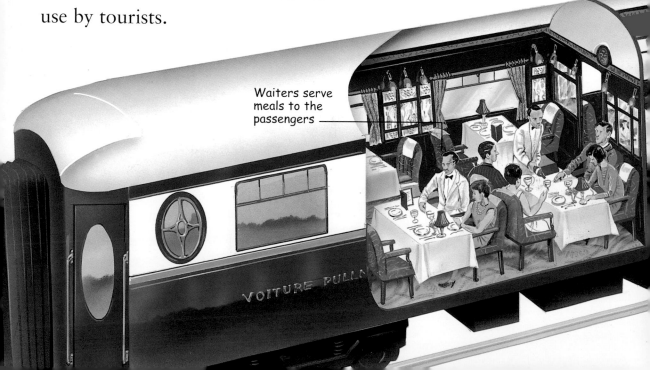

Waiters serve meals to the passengers

VOITURE PULL

Staff on board

The passengers on board the luxury trains are taken care of by staff trained as chefs, waiters, stewards, conductors, and porters.

By day

The beds in the sleeping compartment fold away, leaving a comfortable sitting area.

Decorative panels line the walls

Traveling restaurant

The Lalique dining car, built in 1929 as a first-class Pullman, is one of the cars used on the Venice Simplon-Orient-Express, which runs on routes in Europe. The car is named after René Lalique, who designed its decorative panels.

Powered by diesel

In the 1930s, diesel trains started running in countries such as the U.S.A. and Germany, where diesel was cheaper than coal. Most diesel engines power a generator that makes electricity. This drives a motor that turns the wheels. Like steam engines, diesel locomotives gave off fumes, but were easier to clean and maintain. Some were also very fast. The American Burlington Zephyr ran at an average speed of 83 miles per hour. By the late 1950s, most passenger trains in North America were hauled by diesels. Ten years later, steam engines had disappeared from almost all railroads in Europe and North America.

Longest and heaviest
The record-breaking Union Pacific Centennial diesel locomotive is almost 100 feet long and weighs 229 tons.

Flying Hamburger
The German Fliegende (Flying) Hamburger trains ran between Hamburg and Berlin from 1932. They covered the 178 miles in under three hours at speeds of up to 100 miles per hour.

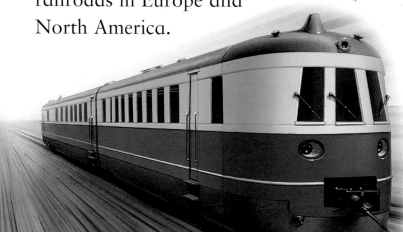

Double the power

Two diesel locomotives, one at each end, power this nine-car, high-speed train that travels at 125 miles per hour between Aberdeen and London in Great Britain.

Pulling a load

Freight trains are often used for hauling goods over long distances. Loads of coal, oil, and raw materials such as steel and timber all go by rail. In large countries such as the U.S.A., Canada, and Australia, trains carry more freight than passengers. Although not as fast as planes or as convenient as trucks, trains can carry huge loads. A 100-car freight train might be 1.25 miles long. To move the same load by road, you would need 100 trucks and drivers.

Bulk carriers

Different types of carriers are used to transport different goods. Large tankers like this one are used to carry diesel and liquid gas.

Covering vast distances

Bulky freight such as coal, oil, and minerals is carried in specially designed wagons. These are often open-topped so that the wagons can be loaded on the move. Each wagon is fitted with its own set of air brakes, operated by the engineer.

Carried by container

Freight is often carried in huge steel boxes called containers. Each box fits on the freight car of a train. When they arrive at the depot, the boxes are then loaded on trucks. From here, they can be driven to the docks and loaded on ships to be transported to other countries.

Container

Cranes lift the containers off the train and load them on trucks.

Freight car

Electric trains

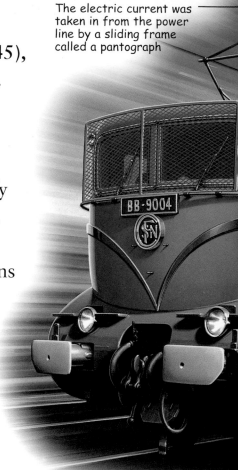

BB-9004

During World War II (1939–1945), many railroads were damaged. Whole sections of track in countries such as France and Germany were destroyed by bombs. After the war, they began to rebuild and electrify the old lines, as well as building new ones. Putting up the posts and wires that carry the power supply is expensive, but the trains run faster and do not produce smoke. Some countries, like Switzerland, have electrified most of their lines.

Early days of electricity

Built in 1895, this electric engine pulled trains through a 1.25-mile tunnel in Baltimore, Maryland. It replaced steam engines, which were filling the tunnel with smoke.

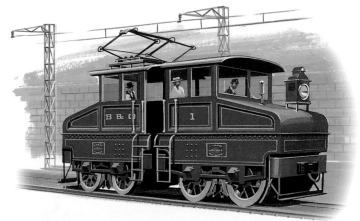

Record breakers

In 1955, near Bordeaux in France, two electric locomotives (CC-7107 and BB-9004), each hauling three coaches, reached a record speed of 207 miles per hour on two different days.

18

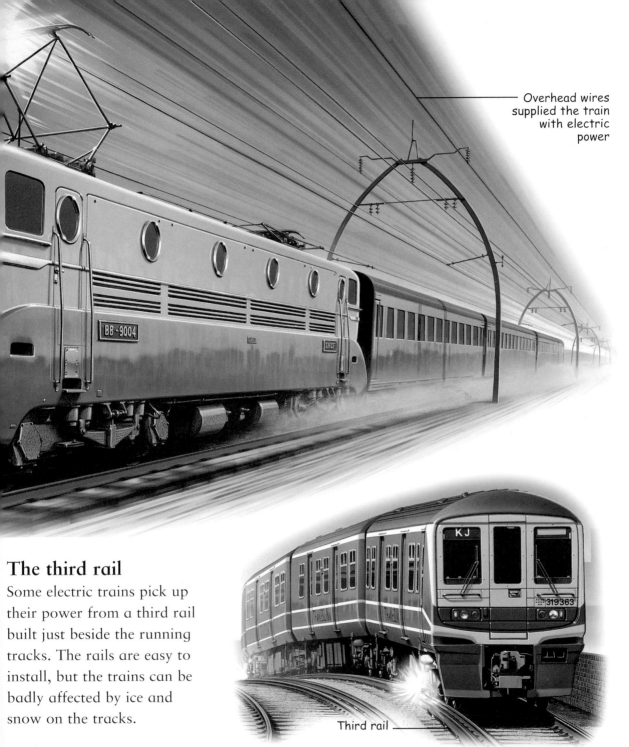

Overhead wires
supplied the train
with electric
power

The third rail

Some electric trains pick up
their power from a third rail
built just beside the running
tracks. The rails are easy to
install, but the trains can be
badly affected by ice and
snow on the tracks.

Third rail

Staying on track

Railroads carry many different types of trains.
Intercity passenger trains running at more than 125 miles per hour use the same lines as commuter trains and freight trains. Trains can move from one line to another by way of points. These are controlled from a signal box or panel. Colored-light signals are used to make railroad systems safe and efficient. They show the engineer which route to take and let him or her know if there is another train ahead or about to cross paths.

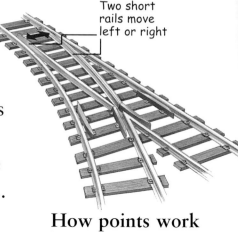

Two short rails move left or right

How points work
When the points change, two short rails that come to a point move from one side to the other. This allows the train to change track.

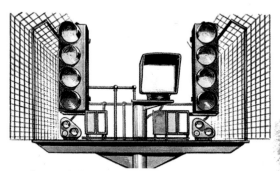

Colored-light signals
A green light means that the line is clear. A red light means stop. Yellow lights warn the driver that the next signal may be red—this is important because trains cannot stop suddenly. The small white lights show that a train is being re-routed.

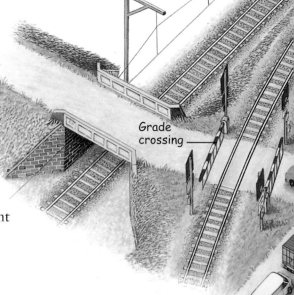

Grade crossing

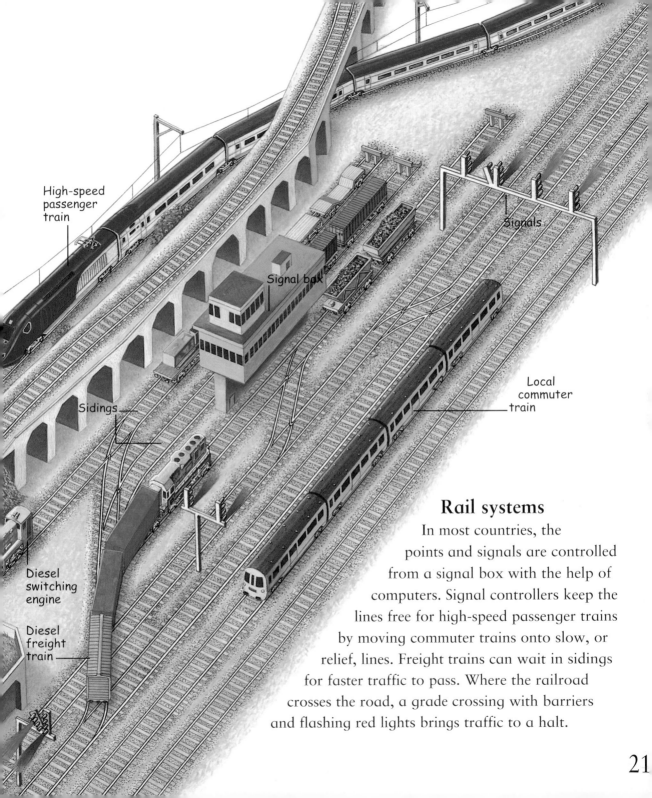

High-speed
passenger
train

Signals

Signal box

Local
commuter
train

Sidings

Diesel
switching
engine

Diesel
freight
train

Rail systems

In most countries, the
points and signals are controlled
from a signal box with the help of
computers. Signal controllers keep the
lines free for high-speed passenger trains
by moving commuter trains onto slow, or
relief, lines. Freight trains can wait in sidings
for faster traffic to pass. Where the railroad
crosses the road, a grade crossing with barriers
and flashing red lights brings traffic to a halt.

Mountain railroads

In northern Mexico, trains cross the Sierra Madre mountain range on a spectacular line that runs 406 miles from Los Mochis near the Pacific coast to the city of Chihuahua. Leaving Los Mochis, the train climbs from sea level to a height of 8,200 feet. At the top, it reaches the Copper Canyon—an area with 10 miles of canyons up to 1.25 miles deep. One tourist train a day makes the 14-hour journey in each direction. The railroad took 90 years to build and was finally opened in 1961.

Rack railroad

On steep railroads, a bar (or rack) i laid between the rails. Like a row of teeth with gaps, it links and grips with a cogwheel under the engine as it drives the train up or down the mountain.

To the summit

The line twists and turns
through 86 tunnels and over
59 viaducts built high in the
mountains. The highest
point, Divisadero, is
perched at 8,070
feet, right on the
rim of Copper
Canyon.

Tunnels and bridges

In hilly areas, engineers have to build tunnels through mountains. They also have to build bridges across rivers and valleys. The lines would be too steep for trains to climb if they followed the ups and downs of most roads. Early tunnels were difficult and dangerous to build. Underground rivers might cause a sudden flood, while breaking up rock with gunpowder could bring the roof down. The longest railroad tunnel runs underwater for 33 miles between the islands of Honshu and Hokkaido in Japan. It was opened in 1988.

Channel Tunnel

Opened in 1994, the Channel Tunnel stretches beneath the English Channel—the strip of water that separates France from England.

Machines bored into the tunnel from both sides of the Channel

Sydney Harbour Bridge

Sydney's famous bridge was opened in 1932. It links two parts of this big Australian city. The main span is 1,650 feet long and gives clearance for shipping of 161 feet.

High-speed trains

The fastest passenger trains in the world run in France and Japan. Both of these countries have built high-speed lines with no sharp bends. They carry electric-powered trains at speeds of up to 199 miles per hour in commercial use. In April 2007, a shortened TGV (*train à grande vitesse*) running under test conditions set a record speed of 357.2 miles per hour.

The French TGV

The TGV first started running between Paris and Lyon in 1982. The journey time was cut from three to two hours. New lines have since been built to link cities all over France and beyond.

The Acela Express

Since 2000, high-speed tilting trains have been racing along at 150 miles per hour between Washington, D.C., New York, and Boston. This has significantly reduced the travel time between these highly populated cities.

The German ICE

These intercity trains run at incredible speeds. A line built in 2006 is equipped for speeds of up to 186 miles per hour. It usually goes slower when carrying passengers, at 124–175 miles per hour.

Italian tilting trains

In Italy, there are tilting trains known as pendolinos. They can run at around 150 miles per hour on existing lines. The cars tilt from side to side as they travel over bends in the tracks.

The Japanese bullet

A high-speed train called the Shinkansen runs in Japan. These trains are also known as bullet trains because of the high speeds at which they travel. The first bullet trains ran at more than 100 miles per hour in 1964 between Tokyo and Osaka. Now, the trains run at speeds of up to 186 miles per hour.

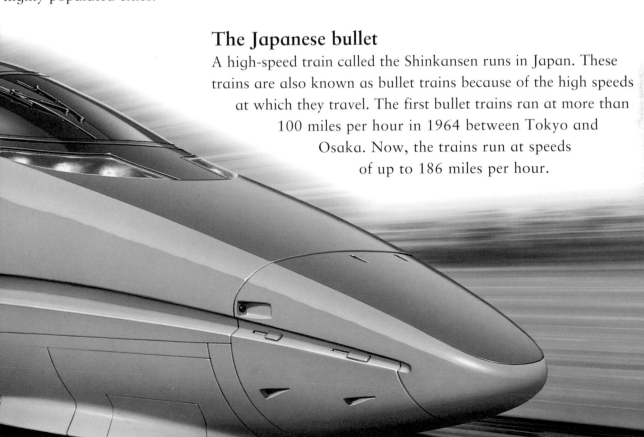

City railroads

Railroads run to the center of many major cities, allowing a large number of people to easily travel downtown from their homes.

Unlike cars, most trains don't give off smoke or fumes, and they are not held up by traffic jams. Large stations such as Grand Central Station in New York are close to shopping and business areas. At many stations, there is an interchange system where people can continue their journey by underground or elevated rail, or by bus, streetcar, or taxi.

Elevated railroads

In some cities like Chicago and Singapore, electric trains run on elevated lines built above the streets. Elevated lines also link different parts of large airports together.

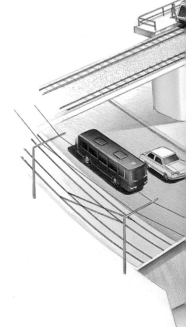

Below ground

Railroads run underground in many cities. They are operated by electricity. The first subway was opened in London, England, in 1863.

Above ground

Streetcars run on steel rails sunk into the surface of the road. In some cities, streetcars provide an alternative form of transportation.

Networking

Well-planned city stations are positioned close to other transportation systems. Stairs and escalators lead down to a subway and up to street level, where there is often a large concourse.

Monorails

"Mono" means one, and monorails run along one rail, not two. The track is usually high above the ground, and trains can hang below the rail or ride above it.

Monorail

Concourse

Elevated railroad

Ticket booth

Subway

Streetcar

29

Maglev trains

The maglev train does not have wheels and does not run on rails. Guided by tracks, or guideways, it seems to run on a cushion of air. In fact, magnets on the train and in the guideways repel each other. This makes the cars float about a quarter of an inch off the ground and also propels them forward. The word *maglev* is short for magnetic levitation (levitation means "rising into the air"). Since the train doesn't touch the guideway, there is no friction to slow it down.

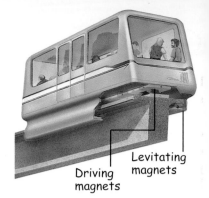

Driving magnets

Levitating magnets

Computer-controlled

Maglevs are sometimes used to carry passengers between the buildings of an airport. These driverless maglevs are operated by computers.

Faster than ever

In 2003, a maglev train in Japan reached the record speed of 361 miles per hour.

Magnets contained in train panels

Passenger door slides up

Guide wheels

Magnets in the guideway

Glossary

bullet train A Japanese high-speed, streamlined train.

car An enclosed compartment on a train for carrying passengers. A car is also known as a coach.

diesel A fuel used to power diesel engines.

engine (1) Any machine that converts energy into mechanical work. (2) A railroad locomotive.

engineer (1) The driver of a train. (2) Someone who builds railroads or locomotives.

flange A lip on the metal wheel of a train that keeps it on the tracks and guides it around corners.

freight Goods transported in large quantities, often by rail.

gauge The width between the two rails on a railroad track. In North America and most of Europe, the gauge is 4 feet 8.5 inches.

generator A machine that makes power or heat.

grade crossing The point at which a railroad and a road cross. It usually has barriers to close off the road when a train passes.

immigrant A person who has recently moved from one country to another.

locomotive An engine powered by steam, electricity, or diesel, used for pulling trains along railroad tracks.

maglev train A high-speed train that runs on magnets located in the train and on the track.

monorail A train that runs on a single rail.

points Rails in the track that move to guide the train onto a different route.

porter A person who carries passengers' baggage in a train station.

Pullman car A luxury car, where passengers can have meals and refreshments at every seat, or rest in a sleeping cabin.

rack railroad A steep railroad that uses a central rail linked to a cog wheel to guide the train up and down the track.

repel If two magnets repel each other, they push away from each other.

siding A short stretch of track connected to the main line where trains can wait.

signals Colored lights used to tell the engineer that the way ahead is clear.

sleeper A wooden block used to support the rails of a track.

span The distance between the two ends of a bridge.

steward A person on a train whose job is to help the passengers.

third rail A length of rail built beside the tracks that transmits electric power to the engine.

track A pair of parallel rails on which trains run.

wagon An open car used for carrying freight.

Index